MAGGIE SIMPSON'S
BOOK OF COLORS AND SHAPES

Maggie Groening and Matt Groening

HarperCollins*Publishers*

Art Direction and Design: Cindy Vance

Critical Model: Mathias Groening Bartlett

Creative Team: Bill Morrison, Ray Johnson, Dale Hendrickson, Peter Alexander, and Steve Vance

Editor: Wendy Wolf

Legal Guardian: Susan Grode

FIRST EDITION

Library of Congress Cataloging-in-Publication Data
Groening, Maggie.
   Maggie Simpson's book of colors and shapes/by Maggie Groening and Matt Groening.
     p.   cm.
   Summary: Illustrations of different objects and members of the Simpson family introduce colors and shapes.
   ISBN 0-694-00320-4 (pbk.). — ISBN 0-06-020235-1 (lib. bdg.)
   1. Color—Juvenile literature. 2. Colors—Juvenile literature. 3. Form perception—Juvenile literature.
[1. Color. 2. Shape.]
I. Groening, Matt II. Title.
QC495.5.G76 1991   91-2864
535.6—dc20   CIP
                                                      AC

YELLOW STAR

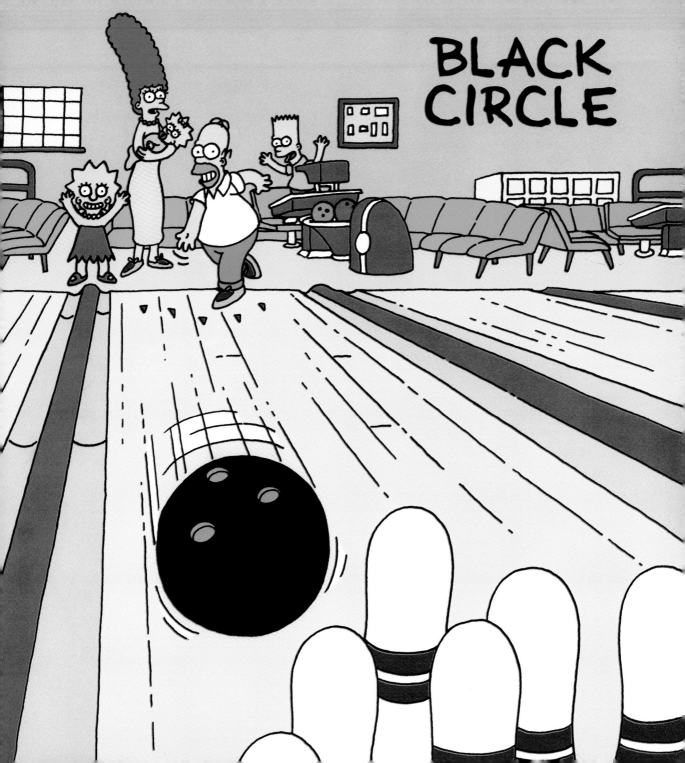

ORANGE
CIRCLE

PINK
CIRCLE

WHITE OVALS

CIRCLES

SQUARES

TRIANGLES

Maggie Groening, the original inspiration for the enigmatic youngest Simpson, writes books for children. She lives in Brooklyn, New York.

Matt Groening, brother of Maggie Groening, is the creator of *The Simpsons*™ and *Life in Hell*®. He lives in Los Angeles.